FINALLY FULL-TIME

bi-vocational bonuses & tentmaker tips

For Kimberly, my full-time friend

INTRODUCTION

"**G**od, send us a poor, humble preacher. You keep him humble, Lord, and we'll keep him poor!"

With tongue in cheek we in ministry joke about what church people might say they are looking for in their pastor:

> *"Someone who works more than one day a week."*

> *"Someone who is 30 years old and has 35 years of experience."*

> *"Someone who understands they aren't part-time, just 'partially compensated.'"*

But what if it were the pastors and preachers who were tasked with building the perfect version of themselves in a "Build-a-Bishop" Workshop? What would the final outcome look like?

Certainly there would be as many particular nuances given to this specimen as there are project contributors, but I'm quite sure that the one attribute common to almost everyone's blueprint would be...

"He must be full-time."

This book makes the case otherwise.

ONCE UPON A TIME
OUT WEST

I was just a 14-year-old, tagging along with my dad to the preacher's fellowship meeting at a church an hour away from our home in New Mexico. There were many preachers present for this overnight event, and several had their wives along with them. Some, like my dad, had a kid or two in tow. Naturally, some of the pastors were full-time and some were bi-vocational. A lot of activity would be crammed into the next twenty-four hours, which were always fast-paced. The exception would be a brief two minute period which for me was so profoundly, intensely disturbing that it seemed to last for two hours.

The big Monday evening opening service included dozens of preachers and their families, most of the members of the host church, and many lay folk brought by some of the nearby pastors. There were hundreds of people there, and it was electric. It stands out as a big event in my formative years, and so I remember a lot. And it must have been winter because I distinctly recall that it was dark outside.

But it wasn't dark inside. Everyone was so happy and bright. They had an aura about them.

Speaking of illumination, the host church was built in the 60s or 70s, which meant the lighting was somewhat dim. It seems to me that many of the churches in those days would build a high wood ceiling with incandescent opaque lighting fixtures hanging nearly halfway to the floor on long vertical rods. The round plastic globes were open at the top and bottom and had decorative metal frames around them which connected to metal grates at the bottom to prevent a broken bulb from falling. That meant the lights inside were free to shine upwards onto the ceiling and also a bit downwards toward the pews, but the grates obstructed much of that light. Of course, very little light could diffuse out the sides, which merely glowed a bit sparsely.

If you have been in church any time at all, you've been in this room. And you know that the most dynamic light present in this scenario is that which emanates forth from the many joyful Christian faces beaming all over the room. This was a place above the clouds...a little slice of heaven on earth. There we were, gathered together with those to whom we could closely relate in life and ministry. God had blessed us all so richly, and our inner light penetrated our shells bursting forth with rays of God's Spirit. A smattering of smiles was only outnumbered by handshakes and pats on the back. Left behind at home were the stresses of the ministry and all worries of the future. Today was a day to mutually shine, basking in the glory of this grand occasion.

And then it happened.

The local pastor was well known and popular, and his church was a lot bigger than the average represented. He was a good host, planning out every detail, including the kind of meals that would be most appreciated by preachers. He had even arranged for lodging for many who had come a great distance.

And, there was an agenda: A big service that Monday night. Then Tuesday's morning sessions would give way to a luncheon, followed by golf in the afternoon for the men, while ladies would remain at the church for a time of fellowship.

But none of these grand plans had a chance to transpire before the most memorable occurrence for me on this day. It was during the opening portion of the service—a call to order conducted by the host pastor, who graciously welcomed everyone and thanked them for coming. We sang some wonderful songs, heard some boring announcements, and considered the day's schedule.

It was at this juncture that he said it.

"I want to honor you men of God." (I'm paraphrasing from my best memory)

> *"And so, if you are in full-time ministry, please stand up. Let's give these guys a big hand of appreciation!"*

He emphasized the words "full-time."

All over the room men stood to their feet with heads held high. My dad stood up. The crowd thundered with applause representing immense gratitude for him and many others. I felt pride in that moment. I was proud of my dad. I was proud to be a preacher's kid. I looked around in wonder.

God had recently called me to preach too. He had told me to serve and be a light in the darkness. But as I looked around I eyed an added bonus: Evidently there's great glory found in being a chosen one. Time moved in slow motion and my brain processed far more thoughts in those moments than it can today. Among them was one sure fact. When I'm a preacher someday I will be <u>full-time</u>!

Not present in my thoughts was something I had heard preached many times--that we don't serve God for the accolades. That ministry is a sacrifice. That you don't do it for the money, and that if you do, the joke's on you because there's not much money in that line of work. Well, none of those truths gained reentry into my conscience during the symphony of praise. In the awe of this monumental moment I thought to myself that surely even the angels of heaven were paying tribute to such giants of the faith.

"These guys are heroes!" the emcee agreed with my silent ponderings. The clapping continued for a long time as I looked around the room. But wait, why isn't Brother Barnes standing? My brain raced with panicked thoughts almost audible. I knew him. He was a preacher from our town and friends with my dad. He was applauding rather than being applauded. The look on his face was one of embarrassment as our eyes met. I'm sure my double-take was annoying and my visage surely showed bewilderment as I turned in my pew and gazed directly at him. His countenance replied, "It's ok." And he looked away and continued clapping and smiling at others standing all around. He wanted me to stop looking at him. My irksome gaze was calling attention to his seated self.

I turned and looked at my dad. I could tell he was honored, but that he wanted to sit down. He partially bowed himself and then slowly took his seat although the applause had barely begun to diminish. He didn't want to be rude, but seemed to hope his move would help abate what was for him an awkwardly long moment.

This prompted me to look around at others who were sitting. Many were no doubt church members, but actually, as I continued tediously staring, I recognized that several of these guys were pastors also. I couldn't contain my curiosity so I tapped dad on the arm and he leaned toward me. "Why are some preachers not standing?" I asked.

He shook his head. "We'll talk later, bud."

The applause finally came to a close. It would resume at the next preacher's fellowship a month later.

A GOOD BIT EAST

B ut let's fast forward a few years. I was a senior at a Christian college. In a few months I would graduate with a Bible degree. And I would receive a diploma if and only if my bill was paid in full. This wasn't a problem for me. I had a hefty scholarship because my dad's position qualified me for the "Parent in Christian Service Exemption." It took care of nearly 30 percent of costs.

But I was engaged to a young lady which I just knew was way out of my league. I mean, I was sure God doesn't make mistakes, but perhaps an angel performing clerical work in heaven accidentally mixed up the paperwork because somehow, in some way, I was becoming the recipient of God's all-time best girl. Looking back, I would like to think that God was rewarding me for being such a fine young man. But realistically I must admit that perhaps *she* had some hidden sins from her past for which she must be punished!

Either way, her remaining tuition bill was sizable, and I realized that it was now my duty to help.

We went together to the business office and looked over the itemization. I noticed that she had also applied for the same scholarship and was denied. I asked the clerk to clarify. Her reply was monotone and as automatic as a grainy, oft used recording. "Is her dad full-time?"

In retrospect, it's quite understandable that a great institution such as this must draw the line somewhere or people might abuse the system. But my cynicism had already been peaked in these regards years before back in New Mexico.

For me, the bottom line was simple. Her family's bill was higher for the same reason Bro. Barnes wasn't invited to stand at the preacher's meeting: Their churches were small and they had to work other jobs. They were bi-vocational pastors...you know, like the Apostle Paul.

> *Acts 18:3 - And because he was of the same craft, he abode with them, and wrought: for by their occupation they were tentmakers.*

PREVIOUSLY, UP NORTH

My father-in-law was saved under the preaching of the great Oliver B. Greene in the 50s. He walked the sawdust trail in a tent revival and was born again and called to the ministry. He sacrificed much to get his theology degree as an adult. He had a wife and a pre-teen (my wife's sister is seventeen years her senior). He worked nights and went to classes by day. He graduated and began pastoring a church for little salary. He continued working a job. God blessed his efforts over the years, and he was called to be the pastor of a church of some size.

He was "Finally Full-Time."

More years went by and God called him to start a new church with just a handful of believers a county away. It was small. He had to go back to work. By now my future wife was alive and in grade school. Her parents' sacrifice continued in order to pay for her to get a Christian education in a town a half-hour away. The cost to attend a church-run school can seem difficult to manage, until you compare it to the price of college. Indeed, her parents were suffering from "maltuition."

My folks felt the injustice. My dad had been a bi-vocational pastor for years before he was "Finally Full-Time." And so my mom and dad helped pay off my fiancée's bill. They considered it a privilege, and they have always honored my in-laws and respected the sacrifices they made for the ministry. My parents knew what it was like to live on both sides of the tracks.

Later on, my father-in-law again became a full-time pastor. But he, just like my dad, never forgot what it was like to sit in the cheap seats.

Now let's tread back west where our story began. I was just a young teen when after that evening's pastor fellowship my dad explained to me that some, not all, full-time pastors don't properly respect bi-vocational ministers. "But make no mistake, Jerry," he said with eyes of conviction, "there will be a very long line in heaven made up of guys like Brother Barnes who will hear, one by one, direct from the Master, 'Well done, thou good and faithful servant.'" (Matthew 5:21)

I didn't realize at the time what I know now, that my dad was describing pastors who are indeed full-time...they are full-time Christians!

WHEN IT ALL WENT SOUTH

I graduated from Bible college, and God's best girl and I tied the knot nine days later. I'm going to skip over our seven day honeymoon and tell you about day number 8. We arrived at our first ministry, a medium-sized church with a sizable Christian school and lots of staff. They were all full-time and so were we. They were teachers in the school and I was an assistant pastor over music and outreach. My wife taught piano lessons, played for the church, and worked with me in my ministries. I was proud to have such a career and to be able to pay the bills doing what I loved full-time.

Our coworkers were all a bit older than us, though definitely young themselves in their mid to upper 20s. They too were proud to be full-time, a fact which they discussed at times. It was clear they were the chosen ones, picked on recruitment days gone by, unlike the poor saps that didn't get a ministry and were off working regular jobs with dismal success. I felt pride swell in my own heart upon hearing their dialogue. I was successful. I was chosen. I was special. My mom was right! And it made be feel superior to many friends with whom I had gone to college.

Just then I felt a twinge in my soul. Was I guilty of the same Pharisaical attitudes I had witnessed as a fourteen year old? I wanted to be better than that. Today I wish it had taken root as more than just a passing thought, for it wafted away as quickly as the Spirit had pricked my heart.

The school administrator was old in my mind--33 with three kids. But even he seemed young compared to the nearly 40-year-old pastor. These guys had been full-time for years, and it showed in their wisdom. They even took in an older former pastor who was down on his luck, making him the custodian. He had been bi-vocational but now had no church at all. How I loved that man and his grateful, humble outlook. He had never been a full-time pastor, but he certainly was a full-time Christian.

So we arrived there on day 8 and had a couple of days to unpack what little we had into a tiny apartment that seemed huge with our few belongings in place. Of the three sets of dishes we received as wedding gifts, two remained boxed and pushed together to form a Japanese-style table on the floor. The third was opened and used as intended. We had no bed, a fact which was remedied by the kind pastor who had graciously brought us on board. He retrieved an old waterbed from his attic and gave it to us, even assisting us in its setup. Then he told us to invest in some sunscreen because we were about to join the full staff on a big houseboat for a several-day retreat on a lake a few hours away.

It was close quarters onboard, with only a solitary bedroom for one privileged veteran couple and otherwise just a bunch of double bunks in another room for all the other couples. (Whether this whole arrangement was a good idea or not is a subject for another book.) You need only think back to your own juvenile days to imagine all the teasing they gave to us newlyweds on board. It went too far. The cheap latex mattresses made as much noise as an expensive polished leather chair if even the slightest move is made by its occupant. Fresh off our honeymoon they had us afraid to take more than even a shallow breath all night long.

And it wasn't just that ribbing that offended us, for they maintained a steady diet of worldly talk, whether about popular music, sinful movies, double-entendre, or their overt insubordination to the ministry leadership. Was this what full-time ministry was all about? Certainly not, for by the end of the summer several other new hires arrived and they were godly and pure and shared our disdain for the others' testimonies. Indeed, we spent much more time with the leadership because they encouraged us in Christian maturity and didn't drag us down. It was good to know that there's nothing inherently wrong with being full-time, as long as you purpose to be a full-time Christian.

When did it all begin to go south for me? My downward progression wasn't a steep spiral like some of those staff. Mine was a slow, subtle slope, almost imperceptible, but one which the devil designs for many pastors like me who wouldn't fall for such blatant obscenity. It was the pitfall of pride, for, even as I chose to be better than my comrades, I was puffed up with the same superiority mindset as they held in regard to their old friends who weren't in ministry. I had only been in full-time ministry for a few weeks, yet I was on my way to being the host of my own pastoral fellowship meeting, complete with a big, bright smile devoid of any compassion for those I viewed as inferiors.

SUCCESS IS GOOD, RIGHT?

A man says, "I make good money, isn't that good?"

No, that might be bad, because prosperity may lead you to feel independent and that you don't need God.

"Well, I've got an education, isn't that good?"

No, that might be bad, because that can lead to arrogance and pride. You may begin to function in your own strength rather than God's.

"Well then, certainly if you have health, you have to admit that's good?"

No, that may be bad, because many people have to be laid out flat on their back before they will look up.

"Now, you can't tell me that being full-time isn't preferred to being bi-vocational."

I must confess I've always preferred it, but the Lord has opened my eyes to a much bigger picture than I ever before recognized.

I spent 25 years in full-time ministry, which most would consider an achievement. What's more, my ministries saw blessings not often seen these days. As an Assistant Pastor in a new location I directed an outreach program in a church which nearly tripled in attendance. Many would praise my efforts, though I sincerely tried to redirect the glory to the Lord, my Pastor, and many other factors which I believed led to that success. As the music director there, I envisioned and directed a Christmas pageant which would see tens of thousands come from far and wide to attend. A lot of people were placing me on a pedestal, and I secretly started to enjoy it. I was still in my 20s, and the crowds were basically saying,

"Jerry has slain his ten thousands." (I Samuel 18:7)

But success is good, right?

The pastor there is one of the greatest men of God I've ever known. He came from humble beginnings and was initially part-time in ministry, spending years serving behind the scenes before his big break. He never forgot from whence God had brought him. And he wasn't jealous of my successes. A phone call one night demonstrated this so clearly. I hadn't been there more than a few weeks when my pastor was able to take an overdue vacation. I was tasked with preaching both morning services and the evening message as well. Three people walked the aisle that morning, trusting Christ as their Savior. Seven more did the same that evening, including the teenaged daughter of another assistant pastor in the church.

I had never been responsible for anything that was so blessed by the Lord, and wasn't sure how my pastor would view it. When I answered the phone and heard his voice, I knew I was about to learn a lot about him.

"Great job, Jerry. I'm so proud of you," he said.

That broke the ice nicely. We continued conversing, giving God the glory, and rehearsing the details of who had gotten saved and the general spirit of the day. Then I stated that before his call I wasn't sure how he would take the news. Looking back on that moment, I realize that the fact that I even broached that subject reveals that I was prideful and fishing for more compliments. Let's hit the pause button. What would *you* say to a brash young assistant in such a moment? I must admit I likely wouldn't be as gracious as he was to me.

Ronald Reagan said, "The nine most terrifying words in the English language are, 'I'm from the government and I'm here to help.'" True enough. And the nine words my pastor said next contained condensed wisdom for the ages.

> *"Your success is my success, because I hired you."*

What was the question again? Ah yes: "Success is good, right?" His response seemed to answer that well enough for me.

So began an amazing relationship that continues today, decades later. His statement on that night would help shape some positives for my future ministry. He taught me that we all stand taller on one another's shoulders, that teamwork is what makes the dream work, and that there's no limit to what God will do through us (or even in spite of us) if it doesn't matter who gets the credit.

The next chapter delves into how that advice led to an international sermon ministry which still today enjoys incalculable blessings. Those nine words changed my life.

If only I had taken to heart nine more words with which he continued...

> *"Perfume--It's ok to sniff it, but don't swallow!"*

He went on to explain that praise is like perfume, offered up by someone who loves you. You can take a little whiff and graciously honor the donor, but don't you dare make the monumental mistake of believing that what they are saying about you is true. Ingest it, if you insist, at your own peril! My pastor knew that God had great things in store for me, and that I was bound to become a Lead Pastor myself. He saw promise and potential but gave wise caution as he recognized that I enjoyed praise a bit too much.

I stayed there a few more years and then launched out as a solo pastor in a very small work. Just 30 people voted me in on my 31st birthday, but God blessed and we were quickly in the triple digits. We were privileged to see a lot of people saved and hundreds of them were baptized. And we stayed, just like we had been taught. We remained there twice as long as any pastor they had before us. The people jokingly wanted to name the church after us. You know-"Shirley Temple."

And success is good, right?

Yes. Success is the goal. But how is success defined? As we continue we will learn an important point:

> *If we forget who we used to be, we will cease to be who we think we are.*

THE SERMON HEARD 'ROUND THE WORLD

J une 6, 2004 = A day that for me will last forever.
For the first time ever, on that day, I posted my
Sunday sermon online. That week several pastors unknown to me contacted the church, asking
if they could use the sermon for source material. I
was honored. I had no idea what God had planned.
Allow me to back up and give some needed detail.

Like most pastors, I wanted to post sermon audio
and video on our website. But we had a deaf ministry with just one married deaf couple, the Hawkins.
It was for them, and with that limited vision that I
began doing something seldom done by a pastor. I
posted my sermon manuscript (text version) along
with the usual audio/video, so that our deaf could
read it, and the *PowerPoint*, because they are a very
visual people. But God had a bigger vision! This
whole story is clearly to the Lord's credit. Only *He*
could do what happened next.

Every week more pastors, missionaries, and other

sermon seekers continued writing in asking if they could use our messages as source material/commentary in preparation for their own preaching. At first there were just a few dozen, then hundreds. We had to set up auto-subscribers and get help with the explosive growth. Today, tens of thousands of subscribers and hundreds of thousands of users download an average of 40,000 free sermons each and every week. And yet it is still for that one deaf couple. (Though today there are many other in their circles who also benefit.)

Why this ministry is named "Grace Notes"

I was sitting in Freshman Music Theory in college when the professor used the term 'grace note.' He said it with a tone which suggested we should know what it was. (Today I know that it is an optional note written in small superscript in a score.) I leaned over to my friend and asked, "What's a grace note?" His response: "Jerry, it's a note we don't deserve."

Any sermon truth we receive is a gift of God's grace, which is unmerited. My fourteen years at Grace Baptist Church in Decatur, IL birthed the sermon ministry known as *'Grace Notes.'* To God be the glory, that first sermon from 2004 has been downloaded more than a hundred thousand times, and in total tens of millions of my sermons from the years which followed are now in circulation. Also, I am consistently the most downloaded contributor out of more than 10,000 who post their messages on SermonCentral.com. (Remember, I am making a greater point. This is all to God's glory.)

These are staggering numbers already, but it becomes absolutely mind-melting when you consider that most of those doing the downloading are pastors who have their own church, whether they run 15 or 1,500. There is no way to calculate the reach God has granted to us. Today we can truly go "into all the world!"

I regularly hear great reports about how God is blessing in my subscribers' churches. For years now I've received thousands of emails from people around the world about how they wish they lived in my town so they could go to my church. Meanwhile, I can't get people in my own neighborhood to even attend one special event. Do I resent the blessings being poured out elsewhere? No. Their success is my success. And it's all a testament to our Lord. My mentor was right. We do stand taller on one another's shoulders if we are willing to collaborate, rather than copyright, and if the only credit is given to Jesus.

June 6, 2004 is for me a very special day. On that day the Lord put into motion what would prove to be my biggest ministry blessing to date. And, since He works all things together for good, His plan included using this very ministry to further reveal both my problem and the solution. And who would be the main players God would use to change my life and make this book possible?

Bi-vocational Pastors

You see, far more than half of my subscribers are "tentmakers" but it took fifteen years for that reality to really sink in. You may be wondering why it took so long to grasp this simple statistic. It's simple. Because it was then that I became a bi-vocational pastor.

After many years of pastoring on a full-time basis, we moved to help my in-laws. My wife's father was in the early stages of what would quickly escalate into a seriously debilitating, life altering illness. We came on short notice and without income. Of course, my long-term church kept us on salary for many months following my resignation, but eventually they got a new pastor, and I had to move forward. I began working as an assistant pastor to a man who would become one of my best friends. I also would travel and preach. But our financial needs were much more than those ventures could provide, so I did something I had never done in my adult life.

I got a real job.

I didn't want to. But I had to. And that is the reality for a majority of preachers today. And I'm so glad the Lord put me in that position.

God used my day job to change my life. I became a better Christian. I became a better soulwinner. I became a better husband and father. I became a better pastor. I had gotten comfortable and lazy, had too much free time, and allowed success to go to my head. I not only sniffed the perfume...I swallowed! God used my day job to fix things.

The Lord used my secular venture to change my outlook. It revolutionized my attitude toward tentmakers. As I began to talk one by one to more than a thousand of my multi-tasking subscribers and study and ponder carefully, I made the judgment that these guys are, by and large, better people than I am, better preachers than I am, and better pastors than I am. The Lord used them to solidify my beliefs about what it means to be truly "full-time" for God.

I'M BI-VOCATIONAL

A ctually, I'm not. As I write this I'm in full-time ministry again. In the last chapter, I told you about getting a day job. I had that for over two years, but not any longer. However, it was long enough to learn the lessons I detailed for you.

When I say I'm bi-vocational, my point is that I refuse to do ministry the way I used to do it. Only the tentmaker mindset will work for me now. All my income may come from ministry, but that doesn't mean I can't still possess what I will call the "Bi-vocational Bonuses." I want to hold onto that edge that made me a better Christian, better soulwinner, better husband, better father, and a better pastor. And as I now spend hundreds of hours talking with my tentmaking subscribers, I have learned to glean from them powerful principles that, frankly, I hadn't gotten a handle on in 25+ years of being "full-time."

By the way, this book generalizes distinctions between preachers who are full-time and those who are not. But there are certainly many exceptions in both camps. For instance, I know many preachers who are full-time in their ministry who are great full-time Christians as well. And I know that just because someone is bi-vocational doesn't mean they automatically have this "edge" I'm detailing. But, overall it is my concrete belief, from my personal experience with thousands in both camps, that many of us full-time guys could really benefit from considering the following principles I've learned from the tentmakers.

Bi-vocational Bonuses

1. They are a light in a dark place.

I too was a light before I got too big for my britches. Over the years I became a professional pastoral pencil pusher. I did plenty of visitation to church prospects who had visited but less and less actual witnessing to lost people. And I justified myself because I had people walk the aisle and get saved in church (though most of them were invited by my congregation). I rationalized that I was doing my job because I got emails every day about people saved when my messages were preached in churches around the world. My own congregants would say I was successful because I baptized a lot of people, but what I didn't realize at the time was that I had unwittingly allowed myself to become something no pastor should ever allow himself to become:

A light in a room full of lights

I was just like that cheering crowd decades before at the New Mexico fellowship meeting...beaming brightly in one another's presence but seemingly oblivious to the darkness outside. Of course, there were exceptions present in that auditorium, namely, a bunch of seated bi-vocational ministers. They had not forgotten to light their world. They did it every single day.

At my lowest point I realized that I actually didn't really know any lost people. I had no one to invite to church. Everyone I knew had a light of their own, much like mine, and it got so bad that now in retrospect I must wonder if even *they* could see my light, since it was so obscured.

When I got a secular job I was reminded how bright my light could shine if only I would venture out into dark places. I led more people there to faith in Christ than I did as a pastor. I prayed with people more than I did in church. I started a Bible study and had better services than I did when the cameras were rolling and I knew a sermon would go viral.

Jesus said it first and said it best: "I am the light of the world."
Jesus made His bold claim of being the light of the world right in front of the temple during the big festival of tabernacles, with a great crowd gathered. At night they would surround the temple mount with candelabras, and the atmosphere was illumined. I believe it was at that time that Jesus spoke John

8:12. It was true 2,000 years ago when He said it, and it's still true today.

In the beginning, Christ was part of the Godhead which said, Let there be light. He was in the burning bush which spoke to Moses and that pillar of fire which led Israel thru the wilderness. The Psalmist said, He is my light and my salvation. He was the light of the world, born at night to dispel darkness with His light. He was the bright light seen by disciples on a hillside at His transfiguration, and the light which blinded Saul the day he got saved. He is the light of heaven where there is no need of sun or moon. The Word of God is a lamp to our feet and light to our path, and He is that Word. I love the old hymn that says, "How beautiful to walk in the steps of the Savior, stepping in the light!"

Our world depicts Christianity as a leap of faith into the darkness, but, the fact is, it's a step into the light!

Jesus illuminates the darkness. And what is darkness? Simply put, it is the absence of light. If you walk into a dark room and you don't like it, it does no good to stand there and curse the darkness. The best thing to do is to turn on a light, and then darkness flees. Biblically speaking, darkness is a symbol of life without God, who is light. To live without the knowledge of God and His Word is to walk in spiritual darkness.

Preachers shouldn't be dim 1970s light fixtures hanging in the church all day. We should purposefully lead by example and get out in the highways and hedges ourselves, letting our light shine in dark places.

Romans 1 says of the world that they profess themselves to be wise and are become fools because they reject God and walk in darkness. Man chooses to walk in darkness because to step into the light would expose him as the sinner that he is. 'Tis better to lurk in the shadows!

Man has always sought the answer to three shadowy questions:

Who am I?
Why am I here?
Where am I going?

The world has no good answers to these questions. And so lost people meander the planet believing the following:

I'm no one special.
I've no real purpose.
I'm going nowhere. (At death I will cease to exist.)

That's not light, that's darkness. People are sucked in like a black hole, having no direction, not knowing where their life is headed, unless and until a beacon appears on a hillside--a lighthouse I say, showing them the way! If only you can answer those three questions, then it matters not if you never even passed grade school, you have more light than all the enlightened PhD's in the world.

You are a light, man of God. Don't hide it under a bushel. Don't let Satan blow it out. Let it shine. And make sure it shines in places beyond your four walls.

I'm reminded of a story about two carpenters. One was always teasing the other, who was not known for being very smart. One night he shined his flashlight up to the second story of a house and said, 'Would you mind climbing up this light beam and getting my hammer for me?'
The nitwit said, 'Hah, how dumb do think I am?'
'I'm sorry,' the first replied.
'You'd better be. I know you too well...you'd let me get halfway up and then turn the light off!'

That sounds a lot like how many of us witness. God opens a door for us to be a soulwinner and about the time we get started we suddenly go out like a light!

God has deposited the light in three places: In the Scriptures, in the Savior, and in the Saints. Let's talk about that last one.

Jesus looked at His crew of common fishermen and blue collar disciples and said, You are the light of the world. The subject of His sentence was in the emphatic tense, meaning, "You and you alone are the light of the world." That's funny, since it was the Greeks that were known as the enlightened ones, not these commoners. Socrates, Aristotle, and Plato had already given their full teachings, and

the Greek's art and architecture gave them place-
ment as the most advanced society. So how ironic is
it when Jesus then turns to this hairy bunch of Duck
Dynasty looking characters and says, "You and you
alone are the light of the world...I'm depositing the
light in you so you can go out to a dark world and
illuminate."

When *Grace Notes* began exploding in growth and
I first began to realize that so many of them
were tentmakers, there was a part of me that
looked down my nose at them. I imagined some
backwoods, uneducated hillbillies in overalls who
couldn't write a sermon. Boy was I wrong. Oh how
God has changed me on this matter. As I have spent
years ministering to these gentlemen, they have
turned the tables on me, giving me so much more in
return.

"I'd rather be a redneck Christian, Lord, than anything I know!"

About those ragtag disciples: Why were they the
light of the world? Not because they in some way
produced light, but rather because they reflected
His light! Even better, the light is *inside* each of us,
so I like to picture myself not as a mirror reflecting
light, but as a glass globe, out of which the light can
shine. I don't want people to see me, but to see Jesus
in me. So it is not the quality of the globe, but the
quality of the light that men see. The more trans-
parent the globe, the better. Those opaque white

fixtures from fifty years ago may glow a bit at best, but they don't diffuse much light from within out into the room.

> *Matthew 5:16 - Let your light so shine before men, that they may see your good works, and glorify your Father which is in heaven.*

These are great days in which we live because they are dark days, and that's when our light can really shine. So, shouldn't we allow the light to venture out from our church sanctuary? Salt in the shaker is accomplishing nothing. If you are a full-time pastor, please remember to be a full-time Christian by journeying out, intentionally, into the shadows.

I remember a church member approaching me and stating something of this sort:
"Pastor, pray for me, I'm one of the only Christians where I work."
I replied, "Okay, I'll pray for you."
To which he said, "Yeah, pray that I get a different job."

What?

That's like a light bulb that doesn't want to be in a dark place. What if every light bulb wanted to be a part of the large fixture display at the home improvement store? They would all be useless, none would have an impact, none would stand out, none would get noticed, and none would make any difference at all. It's time for believers to quit whining and start shining! If I'm right, then shouldn't preachers be leading the way? Or are we content to remain a fixture in the church building, sending others out in our stead. "Do as I say, not as I do."

> *2 Corinthians 4:3-4 But if our gospel be hid, it is hid to them that are lost: In whom the god of this world hath blinded the minds of them which believe not, lest the light of the glorious gospel of Christ, who is the image of God, should shine unto them.*

We full-time preachers need to be full-time secular disciples. It only happens on purpose, because we don't have to daily punch the clock in a dark place. That was just advantage #1, and it's the biggest bi-vocational bonus. Now, briefly, here's a few more advantageous principles to ponder.

2. I've noticed that the bi-vocational pastor usually has better everyday people skills than I have.
Yes, I may have polished pastoral skills with church folk, but there's a difference between pastor skills and true people skills. My day job included a lot of customer service with real people. I'm not saying that church people aren't real but rather that most of them go into a kind of "church mode" when they drive onto the property. At my workplace, no one was putting on airs. I wasn't in the spotlight. I sim-

ply had a job to do. I had to be a servant, not a celebrity. And I noticed that people appreciated that quality in me.

Early in ministry I was a true workman, seeking to do things behind the scenes with no mantle of leadership to don. If I cleaned a widow's gutters then she and I were the only ones who knew about it other than the Lord. I didn't want to sound a trumpet and announce it to the kingdom, and I certainly had no opportunity to post it online and see how much I could boost my reputation with likes, shares, and comments.

Sometimes I think we watch so much politics that we unwittingly become politicians ourselves, making many of our decisions based more on which direction the winds of opinion are blowing...trying to enhance our public persona and build our little kingdom. People today want someone who is real, just like them. They want a level playing field. They need a pastor who realizes that, though he is the local head of the church, in truth, the head is just another body part.

Jesus said he who is greatest will be a servant, and that stands in contrast to being a celebrity.

3. The tentmakers I know work too hard and they are far too busy to play around with sin on the side. Let's recall a simple adage from our youth.

"Idle hands are the devil's workshop."

Almost every day you hear about another "man of God" who has had a moral failure. We hear it so much we grow numb to the gravity of the situation. I'll bet that if you think about it you'll realize, as I do, that the ones who fall usually aren't bi-vocational. Let me clarify that being full-time doesn't mean you are more prone to sin, but the simple truth is that the guys who fall are usually set up for that fall in some way...often because they have more down time with which the devil can do his bidding.

The tentmakers I know don't have much time to dabble in the dark. They run around in survival mode, just trying to get all their work done and somehow be prepared to preach on Sunday, without losing their wife and kids in the process. This is one reason I'm deeply gratified that God has used my online sermon ministry to help the tentmakers' biggest challenge--a lack of time.

We can have a civil disagreement about some of the above, but here's a hill I will die on: When I worked a second job I sinned less.

My devotions may have been abbreviated at times, but they sure were focused and purposeful. I didn't waste as much time with TV, internet, social media, and trivial hobbies.

4. Bi-vocational preachers aren't tempted to pander to big givers.

As far as I'm concerned, there is one primary reason the Lord commanded that it's a bad idea to be a respecter of persons:

Me.

I'm human, like you. And so the sooner we admit that God is right about our sinful tendency toward favoritism the better. The tentmaker certainly has less of this temptation. And it's also to his benefit, for, as we all know, it's difficult to fire a volunteer!

Even a full-timer can take a lesson here. It really is best for the pastor not to be 'in the know' about who gives what. Now there is wisdom in knowing who gives...just not what they give.

5. Lost people can relate to the tentmaker.

You know that wall lost people often put up when you introduce yourself as a pastor? It's a natural reaction for them. In their mind, you are just after their money. You just want their backside to fill a seat. Perhaps they've known a lot of preachers who seemed more like a celebrity than a servant.

The solution: Don't be a pastor. Be a person.

My subscribers all agree that their job gives them opportunities to speak with many folks that they never could spend time with if being a pastor was their only inroad. My personal experience agrees.

Even after my day -job customers would find out that I am a preacher, I still sensed little to no wall obstructing their view of the truth, because I was relating to them as a real person, and I was willing to leave my throne (fort of safety) and walk among the commoners as one of them.

I have purposed to cling to these bi-vocational bonuses even now that I'm full-time. I want to be a full-time Christian.

Every believer is the best Christian that *somebody* knows. Are you content with all of your "somebodys" being other believers? Let's get out into the darkness and be known to the lost as well. Let's have two vocations. I want to be both a *pastor* as well as a *person* who is a disciple of Jesus Christ.

I'M FULL-TIME

Actually, I'm not. I'm bi-vocational. Though all my income comes from ministry, and I don't currently punch a clock in any other ventures, I have purposed in my heart that better than being a full-time spiritual leader is being a full-time follower of Jesus. A key to being a true full-timer is found in not just being a pastor, but also being a regular person.

I must get out into the community for purposes other than just growing my kingdom (the church I pastor). I must be about the kingdom of God, which includes interacting with people who could never possibly benefit the local ministry I lead. Jesus has called me to be a fisher of men. I cannot rest content in being just a keeper of an aquarium.

This calls for another illustration:
Let's use the word "shepherd" in the place of pastor. We can all agree that one thing all pastors have in common, whether they are full-time or tent-makers, is that they are shepherds (sheep herders). Christ is called the Chief Shepherd. We are under-

shepherds.

Now what is it that has qualified you to be a shepherd? And before you go off on a deep theological discourse about your calling and qualifications, just know that I am asking in the most basic sense. Remember, we are pulling this illustration straight out of the pasture.

Let me tell you the first and most entry-level qualification one must meet in order to be a shepherd...

He must be a sheep.

I am a sheep. If you've been born again you are a sheep. May we never forget this all-important component of our being. We are sheep! And it's a very good thing we are, for here is another life-altering truth which has recently roused me out of my spiritual slumber...

Shepherds cannot produce sheep. Only sheep can produce sheep.

Of course I know that theologically speaking only God can give birth to a baby believer, and that only the Lamb of God can regenerate the soul of a human, making them His child. But He has chosen that the method of reproduction forever shall be one sheep reproducing another sheep.

We can make the same point using the picture of

the church being the Lord's body. He's the true head, but has chosen pastors to be the 'local head' of the body. So what basic qualification must anyone meet in order to become the head of the body? They must first be a body part. When we get saved, we are given our place in the body. That's all the head is... just another body part. The role you are instructed to play may include a leadership function, and it may be deemed as important in the eyes of most, but it is not more important than other body parts. To view the head as being "all-important" is a celebrity mindset. And though the head may sit 'atop' the body, when a leader assumes the proper posture of service and humility it's then that we find him prostrate, face down...the head on level ground with the rest of the body.

And so let's revisit the way we often think of ourselves. Am I a preacher, in the most fundamental sense, or am I a person who preaches? A pastor doesn't lead a soul to Christ. A person does. Now if that person happens to be a pastor then that's just fine. The new convert needed to be introduced to the pastor anyway!

Let's get back on level ground. We like to say that the ground is level at Calvary. I tell my church that we must be a place where everybody is somebody and nobody is anybody. I am ashamed to confess that sometimes I have preached that in an attempt to prevent some members from attempting to rise to some inappropriate prominence. Today I have a new mind. Now I'm saying that perhaps *I* was that ascension-minded member all along.

I want to be full-time, and that means being a full-time Christian. I should do what I do, not for a paycheck or in response to the expectations of my title, but rather because I'm a believer…a disciple… a body part…a sheep. And if, in God's plan, *this* sheep has the privilege to be a shepherd (no matter my pay grade and whether I also must make tents) then I'm among the most privileged people to pace the planet.

I'm happy to announce that I'm finally full-time!

Made in the USA
Lexington, KY
25 November 2019

57620143R00026